Witch' in the City

The Witch in the City

Are you a witch?

Tudorbeth

Tudorbeth © 2013

All rights reserved.
No parts of this publication may be reproduced, stored in a retrieval system, or transmitted in any form or by any means whatsoever without the prior permission of the publisher.

A record of this publication is available from the British Library.

ISBN 978-1-907203-63-3

Typesetting by Wordzworth Ltd
www.wordzworth.com

Cover design by Titanium Design Ltd
www.titaniumdesign.co.uk

Printed by Lightning Source UK
www.lightningsource.com

Cover images by Nigel Peace

Published by Local Legend
www.local-legend.co.uk

Dedicated to my mother.
Thank you for the magic and for your love.
Thank you for teaching me about Spirit.
May angels always walk with you.

Blessed Be

About the Author

Tudorbeth is a hereditary practitioner of the Craft.

The rules, philosophy and gifts of Wicca have been passed down to her through several Celtic and English generations.

Born in Wiltshire, she has an Honours degree in Religious Studies and has lived and worked in California and Italy, before returning to live in north London.

Her ancestors' wisdom and knowledge are passed on to you in this book, describing what it really means to be a witch in our modern world.

Contents

Do You Want to Be a Witch?	1
The Goddess and the God	3
Bell, Book and Candle	7
The Pentagram	11
The Altar	17
Casting the Circle	21
The Festivals of Life	23
A Wiccaning	27
An Awakening	35
Hand Fasting	39
The Elder	43
The Funeral	45
Herb Lore	49
Spells, Incantations & Charms	55
Familiars	59
Warlocks, Broomsticks, Scrying ~ Oh My!	63
The Witch Trials	67
Reincarnation	71
Coven or Solitary Witch?	73
Initiation	75
What Kind of Witch?	79
A Witch's Dictionary	85
To Come in this Series	95

Do You Want to Be a Witch?

Dear Reader,

In this book I want to tell you about what it means to be a witch. The term has many meanings and many of our perceptions of it relate to darker times in our history. Let us try to see beyond our misconceptions of the term witch and bring it into the twenty-first century. A witch is not just a person dressed up for Hallowe'en! The Craft is a belief system, a way of life that resonates with strength and protection for everything in this world and the next.

I want to walk with you through this life and show you the different stages of our lives. I want to describe the essentials that are needed and the extra protection we can create for ourselves when things get rough. *The Witch in the City* will show you our ways that have grown throughout generations of men and women, and how to live in today's busy world while still holding onto and recognising the past traditions.

I shall dispel some myths along the way. But always, dear Reader, your path is known only to you. To be a witch is an honour, a blessing, a great responsibility (and at times a curse).

The best way of describing a witch is that we have no problems with anyone, even though they may have problems with us. We are neither white nor black, we are neither good nor bad. We encompass all and do not impose our will on anyone else. Instead, we always try to help and heal as best we can. Sometimes, though, we must walk away in order to protect ourselves and our loved ones.

2 | THE CRAFT IN THE CITY

Do you feel a calling?

To live the life of a witch or finally to become one is not to be taken lightly. Although you are in control of what happens and how you live your life, to be a witch in this modern age can still be dangerous; so I would add a cautionary note about whom you talk openly to. You will know in yourself if it is the right thing to do, as there is no-one better able to guide you spiritually than you yourself.

I have put Initiation at the end of the book so that you may first see our Turning Wheel of Life and what life as a witch might entail. The ceremonies described can be used as a guide and can be enacted outdoors or inside. Living in a city, we may not have a garden but the Craft survives in the smallest of places for it is within us.

There is no doctrine or set of beliefs other than our Witches' Code, or the Wiccan Rede:

"An it harm none, do what ye will."

This is a very strong code and it is the only one we live by. Therefore, to walk the path of a witch, responsibility must be your constant companion. If we break that code then whatever we send out will return back to us threefold. So remember, safety first! Act and spell-weave responsibly!

I do hope you enjoy *The Witch in the City* and that it answers the questions you may have had concerning witches. Let us begin.

Blessed Be

The Goddess and the God

Dear Reader,

There are many aspects of being a witch but one in particular is extremely important. It is the one that guides your way, that calling within you - the spiritual. Traditionally we have acknowledged the Goddess in all her many forms. The Goddess was Gaia, Minerva, Hecate, Aphrodite among many others. We also acknowledge the male, the Lord God, Herne the Hunter, the Green Man, Zeus or Jupiter et al.

Spirituality is something that is deeply personal to you as a witch if you know you have a calling. You will prefer to be out in nature, you care for animals, you believe in magic and like to create spells, you want to look into the past and the future, and 'the other side' is calling... it is the Craft.

Yet what of the Goddess and other deities? In the Craft we change and adapt, we follow our own paths; some of us acknowledge all deities, some follow none but acknowledge the all-encompassing power of the universe. On your altar you may have an image of the Green Man or of a Goddess. If you are unsure about this and do not feel a connection to deities, then on your altar will be items you do have an affinity with, like plants or crystals that may mean you are 'an Earth witch'. An Earth witch is someone who cares for the Earth, as we all do, but does not feel the need to have an image of a deity as representative of the Earth. You may not need to pray to the Goddess, for we all worship and pray in our own personal ways.

However, there are coincidences that may seem to happen. For example, you might constantly be dreaming of a particular animal, or you always see a particular animal or a certain tree where you live. Then it is highly likely that a god or goddess is trying to send you a sign that they are there for you and that you are under their watchful gaze. If you dream of the sea it could be Neptune, Poseidon or even Aphrodite.

Yes, witches (or the 'wise ones', which we were also known as) are aware of all. There are signs all around us and as witches we learn to notice them. As 2012 came to a close there was a terrible plague among our ash trees. Well, in Norse mythology the Yggdrasil is an immense tree that is central to the universe as 'the nine worlds' exist upon it. The Yggdrasil is also known as the tree of Odin and, yes, it is an ash tree. How strange and symbolic that our ash trees were being ravaged right at the end of this era as Yule, or Midwinter's Day, 2012, signified a spiritual turning point for many people.

Being a witch, one is connected to everything. We must be aware of all and know many things; it is not just the culture we come from but the culture that made us. In Britain, our influences include Celtic and Druid, Greek and Roman, Angle, Saxon and Viking. Those old voices can still be heard through our new city streets.

And in city and town parks, the trees still call to us. Keep a sharp look out for the signs as they are still everywhere. The Goddess and Lord God are still here amongst us. But remember, your spirituality is entirely yours and no-one else's.

If you would like to know about the Goddess or God, or you would like to work with a deity, always be respectful. Before you go to sleep, say a little prayer spell:

> *Oh Blessed Deity, whose name I do not know,*
> *please make your presence known*
> *in my dream this night.*

*Let me see you in my sight.
An it harm none, so mote it be.*

The God or Goddess may not come through with a full-blown personal introduction! Instead, they may send you in a dream an animal that is associated with them. Later in this book there is a list of animal correspondences and the deities they correspond to. Remember that deities are powerful so please be very respectful and always use caution when asking them to help you in spell work. This is a privileged part of the Craft to work in.

Blessed Be

Bell, Book and Candle

Dear Reader,

There are many items that have been passed down through the centuries regarding witches, but three in particular are the bell, the book and the candle. The term 'bell, book and candle' also relates to the excommunication rites of the Church towards someone who had committed a non-redeemable sin, so be careful when referring to it. It has been used since medieval times in relation to witches and our practices.

The candle and the art of candle magic, as well as the making of candles, are described in detail in my book *The Craft in the City*, so the discussion will be minimal here. However, it is important also to speak about the bell and the book.

The bell represents the element of air and it is used in ceremonies to summon energies. The bell also marks the beginnings and endings of ceremonies and other things. Traditionally, many years ago during thunderstorms church bells were rung to disperse the darkness. Further, some use the ringing of bells to clear a house of any unwanted guests, such as ghosts or spirits.

In the Craft, the bell represents the feminine principle and is often used to invoke the Goddess in a ritual. Bells also symbolise the voice of the Goddess, so its ringing brings the divine attention to you and vice versa. Bells are used for healing and also for cleansing, including ridding a place of unwanted energy. It may be put on a special shelf, or on your altar, or hung on a door so it can guard the home.

Due to its connection to the divine, the bell is also representative of the spirit. In the Craft everything is connected to the five points of the pentagram (see the next letter) and the wand, the Athame, the chalice and the bell all have their relevant areas and importance. The wand corresponds to air, with yellow candles; the Athame represents fire, with red candles; the chalice is for water, with blue candles; the earth is the pentacle and is of course green. The bell is for spirit and is used with a white candle.

Usually these objects will be passed down through the generations, or you could ask a friend to buy you a personal bell. They can come in all shapes and sizes. You could be walking past a second-hand store or charity shop and see a bell that just seems to 'ring' out to you...

The next object to have is 'the book', your Book of Shadows. Some call it the Grimoire, but sometimes this can refer to the dark arts version. The term originated from the old French 'Grammaire' which was used to refer to any book written in Latin. So really it is not an evil magical text book at all. Instead, we will refer to your book here as a Book of Shadows. In my household, mine has become known as the BOS!

The BOS is a collection of all your magical recipes, and records of the festivals and rituals. It is basically a magical diary and it belongs entirely to you. Always be careful to whom you show it, and keep it secret if you so desire.

The candle, of course, is symbolic of many things: the light of the world, the eternal light of the soul, the light of the Goddess. Candles are used in ritual, in spell work and for ambience. In spell work, candles absorb personal energy and as they burn they are releasing that energy into the universe. All candles have sacred colours that pertain to the deities, and all candles have colour meanings when used in spell work. Always make sure you are aware of the colours and their meanings and intent before doing any spell work.[1]

---

[1] See *The Craft in the City* for detailed correspondences.

The bell, book and candle are a witch's utensils, along with the pentagram, and these are still very important to us. They can be represented in many forms since it is up to you how you wish to follow the Craft and what type of witch you become.

Blessed Be

The Pentagram

Dear Reader,

I need to talk to you about the pentagram and the pentacle. There are many symbols in magic, none more important that the pentacle and the pentagram. The pentacle is a five-pointed star within a circle while the pentagram is the five-pointed star itself. It is sometimes known as 'the star pentagon'. The first recorded data pertaining to the pentagram was in Mesopotamia over 3,000 years ago and it also appears in Sumerian and Babylonian texts.

There are many meanings and usages for this magical image. Pentagrams appear everywhere - in Mathematics, as magical objects and of course in the suit of pentacles in the Tarot. Yet it is magical power we are concerned with here. The pentagram and its five points represent the elements earth, air, fire, water and spirit. We keep it in view always during spell-weaving and rituals. If there was such thing as a Witch School then learning to draw the pentagram would be the first lesson!

First, a word of warning: the pentagram must always be in the upright position, pointing towards the sky, because with magic it is 'as above, so below'. If you see a pentagram with a single point downwards, that is in direct opposition of everything we believe in and work with. The downward pentagram is often used as an anti-Christian symbol, being in direct opposition of Christ. But in fact the pentagram we use predates Christianity by a couple of thousand years.

However, I need to clarify that the pentagram I am going to show you is called the Pentagram of Air. There are other types, the Pentagrams of Fire, Water, Earth and Spirit. Different covens have their own versions and different ways of drawing them. Ours is drawn in the air using the index finger, which is our finger of power, or our 'wand'. We do this to invoke protection, respect and grace; we are protecting ourselves from energies that may do us harm. This is the pentagram of ceremonial and practical magic.

To draw the pentagram is not easy and takes a bit of practice, but the more you draw it the easier it will become and soon it will be second nature. When we learn to write in school, we learn to trace the letters in the air with our finger, and this is exactly how we learn to draw the pentagram. And we have a little rhyme that goes with it to help us remember it. But don't be concerned about the true geographical directions of the compass here - we are just learning how to draw the pentagram quickly, five points with one manoeuvre.

So how do we draw one? It is drawn with five straight strokes or lines. When casting, we learn to draw it in one motion and we actually start at the bottom and then reach for the top. As above, so below.

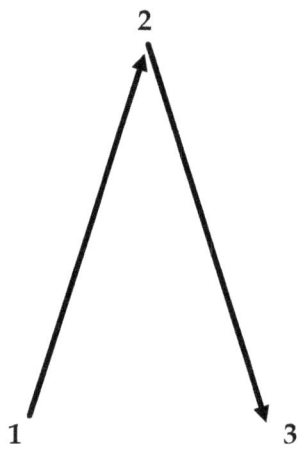

We say, " As above so below..."

When you draw it, it doesn't have to look perfect; this isn't geometry, this is magic and witchcraft. The symbolic shape is a sign of protection, magic and work for the greater good. Each point is associated with a point on the compass, each point resonates with the energy of the element it pertains to, and each element represents a facet of human nature.

Here's the full diagram and the complete rhyme:

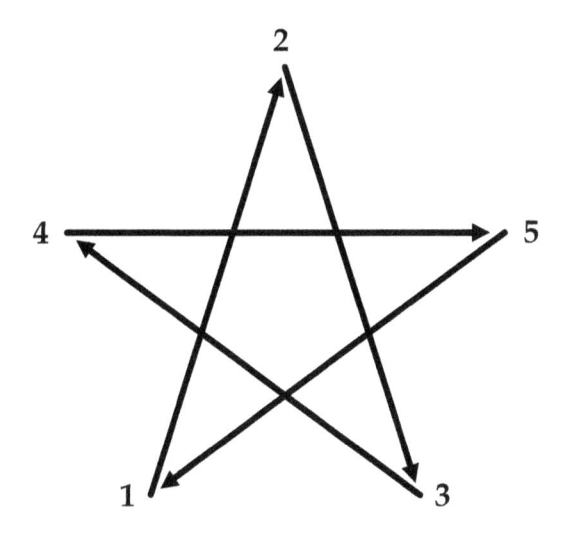

"As above, so below, east west north we go."

1…..2…..3…..4…..5…..1…..

When we draw the pentagram it is entirely about 'drawing down the quarters' and creating our own spiritual nexus within our home or within our own locality. It is for protection and connection to the divine, a symbolic gateway to our spiritual centre.

The starting point (1) is associated with the element of earth, the direction north and the season of winter; this is the material world of possessions, work, values, morals and physical security.

The highest point (2) represents the spirit, of course, and all things of the higher realms.

The element of fire is in the south and at point (3) of our pentagram. It is associated with action, passion, creativity, enterprise, belief and the season of spring.

The element of air is to the east, at point (4). It is associated with the season of autumn, with ideas, communication, truth, and both struggle and justice.

Our final point (5) on the pentagram is for the element of water, the season of summer and the direction west. It is associated not just with love but with all emotions, moods, dreams and fantasy.

We need to have the pentagram around us always in some form. Some of us have a piece of jewellery with it on, worn hidden from plain view if we haven't come out of the broom closet yet. Some may have a tattoo of it somewhere on their person, while others may just have a wooden image to be used for ceremonial purposes. In my book *The Craft in the City* I mention looking to nature to find it. For example, cut an apple in half and there it is. The apple is the fruit of knowledge and love, often being associated with Aphrodite, the goddess of love.

Practise drawing your pentagram. We use it in many ways, drawing one in the air with our wand or with the index finger, at the beginning of a ritual or when spell-casting. It can be used for added protection if we are confronted with something negative or, for example, if someone comes into the office and leaves 'an atmosphere'. The more times you draw one the quicker you will be at creating it. It is our connection to magic, to the Craft, a reminder of who we are and what we inevitably work towards - the greater good and the light of love.

Blessed Be

Here is the pentagram with its associations.

Remember that you are seeing it as if it were drawn in the air in front of you.

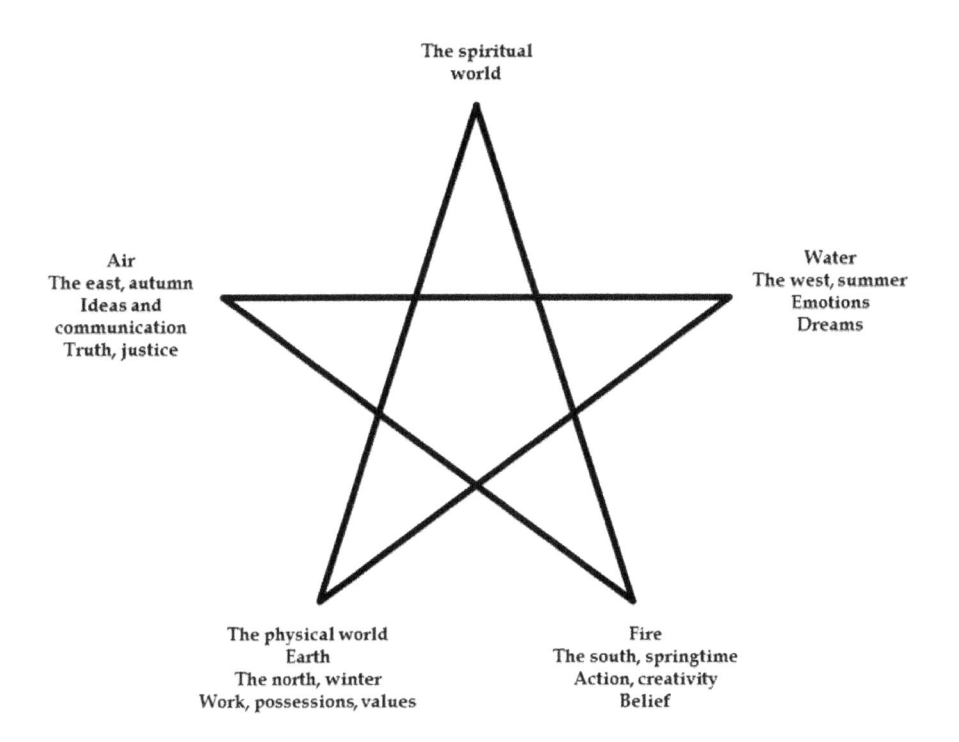

The spiritual world

Air
The east, autumn
Ideas and
communication
Truth, justice

Water
The west, summer
Emotions
Dreams

The physical world
Earth
The north, winter
Work, possessions, values

Fire
The south, springtime
Action, creativity
Belief

The Altar

Dear Reader,

We may live in a house, an apartment or in one room, but nowhere is too small to create a sacred space, a place for an altar. For many, that word conjures up images of stone tables adorned with the paraphernalia of ritual; if you are that lucky, good for you. However, for the majority of us a simple corner or even a shelf is quite sufficient to reconnect on a daily or weekly basis with ourselves and just to centralise our thoughts for a brief respite. We all need somewhere, a little place, a little something that is ours and can be used for peace, meditation, spell-weaving or simple gratitude.

On the altar we can perhaps keep an image of the past, such as a print of a seer or a witch in the old days. For an object of the present, think of nature and the time of year. If it is autumn then maybe a horse chestnut; if it is October then a pumpkin or an image of one, or something that represents Samhain, Hallowe'en.[2] Every month there is a festival, so the future can be represented by having something on your altar for a festival to come.

Also on the altar we would have a pentagram, and an image of a god or goddess we follow (or even a simple image of a fairy representing nature spirits). The Green Man features on mine, as does the stone of Atlantis.

---

[2] The festivals of the year are discussed in detail in *The Craft in the City*.

Our altars are sacred and personal to us but items on it also represents the elements. A seashell can represent water, a plant can represent the earth (or an acorn or chestnut), a candle represents fire, and incense can represent air as does a feather or a fan. If you need a wand then this also represents air; it's a phallic symbol associated with male energy, whereas the cauldron is traditionally female and represents the Goddess. You may have a chalice or special cup you use in your practice, and this also represents water and female energy. Although this is your altar and everything has a meaning for you, these are some items that have been used traditionally and some of us continue to use them.

Now that we have the objects on your altar, we need to consecrate it. You can use holy water or magical salt, or you can consecrate it by air using incense or a smudge (sage) stick to cleanse the area. Waft the incense around your altar while saying:

> *Sacred space, sacred space,*
> *I welcome you into my heart and into my home.*
> *Help me focus my energy*
> *and all good works I do for friends and family,*
> *to all forever.*
> *Blessed Be*

Perhaps your altar itself can be made of materials that represent the elements. Mine is made of driftwood collected from the beach, so it is both wooden, which is of the earth, and also from the sea, the greatest of all water representatives. Further, the wood has been dried by the air and the powerful sea salt within it cleanses it constantly.

We need an altar, our place where we can concentrate. Think about the space you have: is there somewhere that you can have an altar? It is just a little place where you light a candle or two and recognise the past, present and future, creating good thoughts, meditating and casting spells.

Creating your altar is all about you, so put items on it that appeal and that are special to you. Be imaginative and enjoy making it.

Blessed Be

Casting the Circle

Dear Reader,

The casting of a circle during ritual and spell work is important. It is for our protection and focus.

Yet there are at times when we just need to make a quick spell or an affirmation for something. We can't exactly cast a circle in our office or in the supermarket. So instead, you can just imagine a white light of pulsating energy around you and then say the spell for your planned intention, or to acknowledge 'the turning of the wheel' during one of our festival days.

You can cast a circle with salt, using either magic moon salt or normal sea salt. As you go round casting your circle, imagine a white psychic wall coming up around you. This is protecting you because nothing can touch you within the circle of light.

Inside the circle there are normally five candles: red for fire, yellow for air, blue for water, green for earth and white for spirituality. There is also the pentagram and a dish of salt. To extinguish the circle after you have finished your work, thank the elements and blow out the candles one by one.

There are many ways to cast a circle but being a witch is not meant to be complicated - our lives are complicated enough! Make rituals and spells as easy as you want, for you are in control.

Blessed Be

The Festivals of Life

Dear Reader,

You may already be aware of the different festivals of the year, from Samhain through to Mabon. If not, here is a brief rundown of them:

- ☆ *Samhain*　October 31st
- ☆ *Yule*　December 20th – 23rd
- ☆ *Imbolc*　February 2nd
- ☆ *Ostara*　March 20th – 23rd
- ☆ *Beltane*　May 1st
- ☆ *Litha*　June 20th -23rd
- ☆ *Lammas*　August 1st – 2nd
- ☆ *Mabon*　September 20th – 23rd

But you may also be wondering about the different practices we have for celebrating 'life festivals', such as birth, marriage and death. The Turning of the Wheel of the year is just the same as the Turning of the Wheel of life; and just like other religions and belief systems, we too have celebrations to mark significant times. These will be described in more detail in the following chapters.

Let us begin right at the beginning of life, with the Wiccaning. It can be called other names, such as Saining or Paganing. Basically it is a baptism for infants and babies, a naming ceremony or a welcoming rite. It is not an indoctrination; our belief system is a two-way path, for the Craft finds you and you in return find the Craft.

Welcoming a child by a Wiccaning ritual is asking the ancestors, the Goddess or God, and the parents to protect and look out for the child until they reach the next stage. By then it is their choice, as it would be for a confirmation, a bar- or bat-Mitzvah or a coming of age ceremony.

This is usually done at the age of thirteen and it is always the young person's choice. For a girl, it is stepping onto the path of the maiden, the beginning of the path, the lineage of the Sacred Three: maiden, mother and crone. For a boy, he is becoming a man on the path of the male lineage: youth, father and elder. The old term used for a youth was 'hunter' since that was the tradition - the male went out to hunt and provide for his family - but times have changed. Yet ironically, even though the names are different for the male and female paths, the actual ceremonies and the responsibilities that are asked of the maiden and youth are very much the same. The gifts given may be somewhat different too, but the intent is the same.

The next stage in a person's life is a wedding or hand fasting ceremony. This is not something to be taken lightly for it is not meant to be just for this lifetime – the two souls are entwined by a cord for eternity.

There may then be a ceremony for a woman either to help her conceive or for giving thanks after becoming a mother. The same is true for the father, also to give thanks; this ceremony can be done with both parents together.

Some women later have a ritual to mark a very special stage in their life, the menopause. They may even refer to it as a 'womb funeral'. However, we will not discuss this here as it tends to be a very individual choice.

Therefore, the next stage for both man and woman is when we become grandparents. Women enter the final stage, that of the crone, while men become elders. The crone and the elder are both special occasions in one's life and they should be acknowledged, usually with very personal gifts. The timing of this ritual can be at the same time as a Wiccaning for the first grandchild for either the crone or the elder.

Some may not like the term crone, so the Craft may change again for a new generation and, instead, the woman may also become known as an elder. There are so many meanings placed upon words and names describing men and women that one never knows if someone will be offended, but for now I shall retain the old terms. The future will determine where the Craft will lead the names, and how our terminology will change with the coming generations, as no doubt it has done throughout history.

The last ceremony in the Turning of the Wheel of life is that of a funeral. We do not believe in a heaven or a hell. Instead we believe in 'the Summerlands', a place where we can review our lives – yes, lives, for we do believe in reincarnation. In the Summerlands we can choose whether we come back again or return to the source and become a part of the Craft itself, being guides to others and a part of the eternal nature of all. There is a ceremony we perform when we want to let go and connect with the Goddess; it is called 'Drawing Down the Moon'. In my tradition it is followed by 'The Dance of Stars' whereby we give our power back to the universe. More on this later.

These are the festivals of life. In the next few letters we shall look at the actual ceremonies themselves. These can be practised as they are described or they can be modified to suit your own circumstances.

Blessed Be

A Wiccaning

Dear Reader,

In my book *The Craft in the City* I discussed at length the festivals throughout the year that are important to us in the Craft. However, just as there are festivals to recognise the changing seasons - the Turning of the Wheel - we also celebrate too the Turning of the Wheel for our lives, experienced on special occasions. Birth, marriage and death are just some key moments.

In this letter we shall begin at the beginning. In many ways a new birth and a ceremony such as baptism or Christening signifies an acknowledgment of new life and a new hope in the world. It is also a moment of dedication or promise to God that the child will be brought up in that faith.

We have a similar ceremony in the Craft called Wiccaning, or Naming Blessing (blessing of the names). Most people have two names, their surname and their first name. In the Craft, however, we have a third name that is never uttered until the child has reached a certain age. The traditional reason for this was so that the fairies or other mischievous sprites could not exchange the child with a changeling child - a fairy child, a 'child of the fey'. So it is to protect the child from evil. The secret name is only whispered by the presiding priest or priestess into the ear of the babe, so they may recognise their own secret name should they by chance get swapped by a fairy. Many parents choose, for the child's secret name, a name from nature - usually flowers or trees for a girl (such as Rose or

Ash) and animals for a boy (such as Fox, Wolf or Bear). In the Craft, remember, nature is always a part of us.

If you would like to have a naming ceremony, this is what you do. It is usually presided over by the oldest member of the clan or family. If you are a member of a coven then your High Priestess will do this.

If the child is a girl then she will have a 'cummer' or co-mother, though you may refer to her as godmother or goddess mother. If the child is a boy then he has a godfather. The role of the goddess mother or godfather is to protect the child and to be a guardian if anything were to happen to the parents. The godparent is also responsible for the spiritual upbringing of the child, like a teacher or guide. Their role is also to enlist the help of the child's spirit guide and to welcome the angel, god or goddess who presides over the particular month the child is born in. The Craft moulds itself within our lives; some enlist the help of angels while others would ask for the help of a goddess. Each month is looked over by a god or goddess, a tree or plant and an angel. Yes, witches do acknowledge angels. We recognise all.

Here are the months and their chosen deities. This calendar of meanings stems from the many influences we have had here in the northern hemisphere or western civilisation. The east has different months and therefore different names but this is ours, influenced by Roman, Greek, Nordic and Celtic deities.

January
The god Janus, god of beginnings and transitions, usually pictured two-faced since he looks both to the past and to the future.
Trees: birch and rowan.
The angel Gabriel.
Animals: the goose and the otter.
Flowers: the carnation or snowdrop.

February
The goddess Februalia. This is a time to atone for sins, for making sacrifices, for washing and purification.
Trees: rowan and ash.
The angel Barchiel.
Animals: the otter and the wolf.
Flowers: violet or primrose.

March
Mars is the god of war - need I say more?
Trees: ash and alder.
The angel Machidiel.
Animals: wolf and falcon.
Flowers: daffodil or narcissus.

April
The goddess Eostre or Aphrodite, signifying the coming of spring, renewal, rebirth from the death of winter.
Trees: alder and willow.
The angel Asmodel.
Animals: falcon or beaver.
Flowers: sweet pea and daisy.

May
Maia is the goddess of the growth of plants.
Trees: willow or hawthorn.
The angel Ambriel.
Animals: beaver and deer.
Flower: lily of the valley.

June
Juno is the goddess of marriage, motherhood and finance, and the mother of the gods.
Trees: hawthorn or oak.
The angel Muriel.
Animals: deer and woodpecker.
Flower: rose.

July
The god Neptune - Neptunalia is at the height of summer on July 23rd.
Trees: oak or holly.
The angel Verchiel.
Animals: woodpecker and salmon.
Flower: water lily.

August
Diana is goddess of the hunt and the moon; her festival is August 13th. She is synonymous with the Greek goddess Artemis.
Trees: holly and hazel, although oak groves are also sacred to Diana.
The angel Hamaliel.
Animals: salmon or brown bear.
Flowers: gladiolus and poppy.

September
Gaia is the white goddess, the 'Goddess of All' - earth, air, the gods themselves.
Trees: hazel, vine or ivy.
The angel Uriel.
Animals: brown bear and crow.
Flowers: aster or morning glory.

October
The goddess of witchcraft and magic is Hecate. The Romans observed the 29th of the month as her sacred day. Therefore, in my family the New Year begins on the 29th and continues to the 31st October when the traditional Hallowe'en or Samhain begins.
Trees: ivy or reed, although the yew tree is also associated with Hecate.
The angel Barbiel.
Animals: crow or snake.
Flower: marigold.

November
Libinitina is the Roman goddess of funerals. The full moon in this month is called 'the mourning moon'; it is the month of the loss of the day, with the night in the northern hemisphere creeping in so quietly. For us it is the darkest month.
Trees: reed and elder.
The angel Adnachiel.
Animals: snake or owl.
Flower: chrysanthemum.

December
Odin, or Cerunnos, is associated with war, death, magic, wisdom and prophecy among other things. He is celebrated on December 31st, New Year's Eve, a time of prophecy and fortune telling.
Trees: elder or birch.
The angel Anael.
Animals: owl and goose.
Flower: narcissus.

The gifts given to a child for their Wiccaning can be a number of things but usually three in particular: silver, egg and salt. Let me explain: the silver represents wealth, the egg represents fertility and the salt is to ward off evil. However, a modern addition to these is a book to represent knowledge. So some godparents may want to omit the egg and give a book. If it's a boy, I usually give blue moon magic salt, and for a girl it's midsummer magic salt. The silver can be anything from a silver bangle to a silver money box.

The Wiccaning Ceremony

High Priestess or Priest
I call forth through space and time the ancestors of (*father's name*) and (*mother's maiden name*), to bear witness to the recognition of this child into our family. I ask the ancestors to protect and care for this child, whose name is...

Godparent
(*The name.*)

High Priestess or Priest
In this place of worship, of nature and of love, I ask the Goddess and God to bless those who care for this child and grant them your gifts of love, truth and wisdom. So mote it be.

All
So mote it be.

High Priestess or Priest
Goddess of the divine, I ask you to protect this child of nature from all evil. I hereby give this child their soul name.
(*The godparent whispers the name to the Priest or High Priestess, who whispers it into the child's ear.*)

All
Blessed Be.

High Priestess or Priest
We thank the Lord God and Goddess for being with us today to acknowledge this child into our hearts and into our care. We thank the ancestors of (*child's name*) for being present today to bear witness to the recognition of this child. Blessed Be.

All
Blessed Be.

High Priestess or Priest
To those of you present today who testify to protect and care for this child, go forth with love, patience and grace for now and evermore. So mote it be.

All
So mote it be. Blessed Be to one and all.

This ceremony can take place in a garden or indoors. When nature is called for, plants are a good way of bringing the outdoors indoors. The area can be sprayed with holy water made with magic salt, the water being sprayed in a circle prior to the ceremony for protection. The pentagram can be present for protection also, perhaps in an apple; however, more than likely the priest or priestess will have a wooden pentagram in some form.

If you do not know a priest or priestess and are not in a coven, that is fine. You still need godparents but the parent can perform this ritual. After all, you are asking for protection for your child and you are taking control of your life and the festivals of life.

Further, if you feel that you need a Christening as well, that is fine too. We view Christianity, Judaism and other established faiths as societal religions, as groupings of people as it were. Your spiritual belief is still that of a witch. We can have a Christening in a church but we can also have a Wiccaning. We have no problem with that - though some churches may have a problem with us. Therefore, as said previously, do not mention that you are a witch other than to your closest and more trusted friends and only then if they will understand and not judge you. As for a Christening together with a Wiccaning, think of it as spiritual insurance for the child.

Blessed Be

An Awakening

Dear Reader,

After Wiccaning, the next stage of a person's life is that of a girl becoming a maiden or a boy becoming a youth. The young adult is usually thirteen or fourteen and it is entirely up to them if they wish to follow the Craft. Usually a mother or father will perform this ceremony for their son or daughter, depending on whether they have always brought their children up in the Craft. Godparents play a part too, as in this ceremony the young adult's secret name is now mentioned as they repeat it back to the godparents. The gifts are the same as for a Wiccaning: silver, salt and egg (or book). The silver can be a coin or even a silver pen, something that can be kept and used now as an adult.

As the young person is now stepping up to the role of adult and studying has become important, the gift of a book is ever more crucial. The same may be said of the magic salt, which can be any that corresponds to the full moon closest to the young person's day of Awakening. We call this time in life an Awakening because the young person is awakening to the world as an adult and to the Craft, though throughout it is always their choice. If you have brought your children up in nature they will be aware of the turning seasons and the festivals we celebrate. We acknowledge others' but we have some of our own.

An Awakening ceremony can be as open as you want it to be. It can be from mother to daughter, father to son, godparent to their young charge or you can also invite your High Priestess or Priest to do this. It can be a family gathering or just for the parent and child. The ceremony is basically the same for a girl as for a boy. Also, when I write 'parent' here I refer to those previously mentioned who could also perform the ceremony.

The Awakening Ceremony

Parent
Blessed Be to you (*name*).

Young person
Blessed Be to you (*mother or father*).

Parent
(*Name*), you have now reached the age of Awakening. Your life is now beginning its path to adulthood. Are you willing to accept the responsibility?

Young person
I am.

Parent
Then I ask the Goddess and the Lord God to grant you patience, understanding and grace as you travel throughout this life. So mote it be.

Young person
So mote it be.

Parent
I also ask you to help and heal wherever you can and think of those less fortunate, and to honour your ancestors always. So mote it be.

Young person
So mote it be.

Parent
I now ask you, Awakened one, what is your name to give back to nature?
(The soul name is whispered from the godparent into the ear of the young person.)

Young person
I give back my soul name of *(name)* to nature. As an adult now, I promise always to work with nature and protect her whenever I can. Blessed Be to you *(father or mother)*. Thank you for helping me, guiding me as I grow. Thank you to the Earth for her gifts. Blessed Be to all.

All
Blessed Be.

The Awakening is a beautiful ceremony as it gives both parent and child the chance to say things that they may never get to say to each other again. Life goes marching on and in no time our children leave and begin lives of their own. The Awakening ceremony is the last part of our child's journey. As witches, both male and female, we watch and nurture but always let them grow and go.

Blessed Be

Hand Fasting

Dear Reader,

We now come to the ritual of marriage, or what is known as Hand Fasting. Like any marriage, Hand Fasting is not to be taken lightly; but a Hand Fasting ceremony is the joining of two people not only in this lifetime but also for eternity. Therefore, it should always be discussed in detail with your partner if you want or feel the need for it.

A Hand Fasting ceremony, though serious, is a happy and joyful occasion. It is presided over by a High Priestess or Priest, and friends and family can join in. The couple can write their own vows for it - a bit similar to 'love, honour and obey' – but they can change this to correspond to what is important for them.

Usually, the ceremony is performed at sunrise or sunset, when both the moon and sun are in the sky, as we ask for the universe to bear witness to the couple and their love. The members of the wedding party are usually joined together in a circle, and everyone normally has a copy of the Hand Fasting ceremony. Candles are lit and are normally red and pink, for love, romance and passion.

The Hand Fasting Ceremony

High Priestess or Priest
We are gathered here today to unite two souls as one. I ask the Goddess and Lord God to bless this couple and all present with love and grace. So mote it be.

All
So mote it be.

High Priestess or Priest
Hand fasting is a union of two souls for eternity. The golden and silver cords bind the souls together for ever. Do you (*groom's name*) and (*bride's name*) join us here of your own free will?

Bride and Groom
I do.

High Priestess or Priest
Do you acknowledge the eternal bond shared between you?

Bride and Groom
I do.

High Priestess or Priest
Then (*groom's name*) and (*bride's name*) I ask you now to speak the vows you have written to one another. (*The bride and groom exchange personal vows.*)

High Priestess or Priest
Here before witnesses, (*groom's name*) and (*bride's name*) have sworn their vows to each other. With this gold and silver cord I bind them to these vows under the protection of the Goddess and the Lord God, and under the ever eternal watchful gaze of the sun and the moon. So mote it be.

All
So mote it be.

High Priestess or Priest
These cords are not tied, for neither partner is restricted by the other, though connected always together but never restricted by each other. There is freedom to grow. The only enforcement of love is the will to love. So mote it be.

All
So mote it be.

High Priestess or Priest
And now (*groom's name*) and (*bride's name*), recite your oath together.

Bride and Groom
Body to thee, mind to thee, soul to thee, always and forever, so mote it be.

High Priestess or Priest
I thank the Goddess and Lord God for their grace and love in blessing this couple and this wedding party. I now pronounce you husband and wife. Blessed Be.

All
Blessed Be.

The Hand Fasting ceremony is also the time when the newlyweds jump over the broomstick, or besom. Some witches choose to jump over a small bonfire but I think the broomstick is safer. The ceremony can be written in accordance with the wishes of the bride and groom; their vows are written entirely by them with aspects of life that concern them no matter how serious or silly. This is something completely personal for the bride and groom.

Blessed Be

The Elder

Dear Reader.

We mark the stages of life as we honour the festivals of the changing year. It is important to acknowledge them as they are all stepping stones on our life's pathway. Each one is a marker, to rejoice in, to honour and to respect.

Friends and family are with us when we have a party as we become Elders. This can be done at the same time as a Wiccaning. The first grandchild is a symbolic turn of events for us. Traditionally, the woman who had once been a maiden and a mother would now become a crone at the age of about fifty. Yet now, as we change and live longer, the Craft changes with us; so we might say that sixty is the age of the crone or elder – remember, the choice is yours. The ceremony can be presided over by the High Priestess or Priest, or it can be with just you and the family and a small group of friends.

The Elder Ceremony

All

You have wisdom and knowledge, and we ask you to teach us. Guide us with your grace. Show us always how to live in love and respect. So mote it be.

Elder

So mote it be. I am here today in the presence of the Goddess and Lord God, friends and family, to step onto the next part of my life's journey. I have travelled and learned. Blessed Be.

All

Blessed Be.

Elder

I will teach and guide for now and evermore, in the name of the Goddess and the Lord God. Blessed Be to one and all.

All

Blessed Be.

We have now seen all but one of our main ceremonies for the journeys of life, from Wiccaning to Awakening, from Hand Fasting and to Elder. There is one ceremony left, the final one that we commit to, for all our journeys come to an end.

Blessed Be

The Funeral

Dear Reader,

In our modern world, a funeral, wake or passing is a very stressful and sad time for all those involved. Yet we all go through it. For us, we believe it is the next part of an endless journey; we believe in the eternal soul and that nothing ever really dies.

However, before we get to the funeral ceremony there are some things that need to be said. For witches from my tradition in particular there is a rite called 'Drawing Down the Moon'. The High Priestess in a coven may carry out this ceremony to engage with the Goddess, or a solitary practitioner may also do it. It will look very similar to the image on the cover of this book with the woman holding her arms up to the full moon, creating a sort of Y shape. In this context, Drawing Down the Moon is a moment of communion between the universe and the practitioner. It is followed by 'The Dance of Stars' whereby we try to make the stars move. What we are actually doing is giving our knowledge and our power back to the universe. It is a sacred moment between witch and universe, a moment of release.

It is similar to what often happens before people pass away, when our loved ones talk to us not knowing that soon they will be gone from this physical world. For some reason people feel the need to talk to one another; we call this the gift of knowledge. It could be about anything, it could be guidance and it could be forgiveness. In my case, with my grandparents, it was about the history of the family, reminiscing about a family member whom I never even knew; but now their memory resides in me. It is the human soul passing something on to another human being - the gift of knowledge. We as witches not only pass it on to our loved ones but also to the universe by giving back our knowledge in 'trying to make the stars dance'.

A funeral is a ceremony in which the person may be buried or cremated. More often than not witches are cremated nowadays and our ashes scattered in the wind, floated upon the sea or buried back into the ground. The High Priestess or Priest may preside over the ceremony. There is usually a chalice, a cord, a candle and a heat-proof dish, and those attending the funeral will have been asked to write something to the deceased on a piece of paper, if they so wish.

Normally in our modern world the funeral homes organise most things and will ask if you want a church, for example. For us, we usually have our service in a crematorium.

The Funeral Service

The High Priestess or Priest begins the service by lighting a candle.

High Priestess or Priest
Welcome to one and all as we remember and say goodbye to our sister/brother (*name*). We ask the Goddess and Lord God to embrace (*name*) and welcome them home. For all is connected and we return from whence we came. Like the cord that moves into another vessel we move through lives and touch those we meet.
(*The High Priestess or Priest places the cord into the chalice while saying this.*)
So mote it be.

All
So mote it be.

High Priestess or Priest
If there are any of those present who wish to say some words now for our sister/brother, and then come forward.
(This is the time when people who want to say something can do so. They can read what they have written before lighting the paper with the candle and then placing it in the heat-proof dish, or they can just burn the words without speaking as it is something sacred between them and the deceased.)

High Priestess or Priest
And now we say goodbye to our sister/brother.
(If in a crematorium this is the time the curtains are closed and the coffin slips out of sight.)
Blessed spirit, we bid you farewell for you await a new destiny. Blessed Be and go with love. So mote it be.

All
So mote it be.
(The High Priestess or Priest blows out the candle.)

This concludes our ceremonies for the Festivals of Life. They are only guidelines and can be adapted to suit any particular witch or practitioner. I hope you now see that our beliefs are serious; being a witch is not just about herbs, spells or magic.

Blessed Be

Herb Lore

Dear Reader,

We have come to one of my favourite parts of being a witch, herbs and herb lore. Herbs are a wonderful way of reminding us that magic is all around us. It is the one aspect that has survived in its truest form from our ancestors, passed down from generation to generation, from alchemists to chemists to botanists, from Zoroastrianism to Theophrastus.[3]

The medicinal and magical aspects of plants and herbs in particular have been used since the beginning of time. Think of aspirin - it was Hippocrates who knew that powder made from the bark and leaves of the willow tree would alleviate headaches, pains and fevers. Aspirin is now one of the major painkillers in the world and we are discovering more and more about its benefits to our health. Further, the uses of herbs and plants are not limited to the health benefits of humans, as they can be beneficial to animals too. If you do not believe me, and if you have a garden, get a catnip plant and see what happens to the local moggies in the neighbourhood!

To learn all the wondrous aspects of every plant and herb in witchcraft is too large a task for me to describe here. Instead, I will mention some of the more common types and their uses, and some not so common. Try to build up a supply of them as you never know when you may need them. If you live in an apartment and do not have a garden, then dried herbs will

---

[3] A student of Aristotle.

work but the fresh stuff is always better. You could try growing the key ones like mint and basil on your window ledge.

Basil is a great herb, especially good for money spells, so always try to have one growing in your house or garden. Furthermore, catnip is not just good for sending your cats into a frenzy. It's good for humans too as it can soothe digestion and help bring down a fever. Also, we use it in spells for happiness and love. Another all-rounder, though not a herb, is the horse chestnut which features in so many spells and myths that it is simply one of those gifts from nature. Horse chestnuts, also known as conkers, generally fall to earth in October. If walking through a city park be sure to pick some up and keep them on your altar to represent the autumn. Then keep them in a jar for spell-weaving throughout the year. (Incidentally, for some reason horse chestnuts repel spiders so if you do not like spiders, please do not kill them, instead put a couple of horse chestnuts around the place. Remember the saying, "If you want to live and thrive, let a spider run alive.")

Herbs and herb lore can be found in every culture and country throughout time and throughout the world. Interestingly, in an ancient Ethiopian text, the Book of Enoch, the gods reveal the secrets of herbalism not to men but to women. Therefore, in ancient civilisations more often than not it was women who were the first healers and herbalists. Unfortunately, many of the witch trials of women were due to the fact that they were herbalists and practised healing with herbs.

As witches we use herbs not only for healing, spells and with candle magic, but also for beauty treatments, anything from soaps to shampoos and body oils which can be used as moisturisers, as well as in cooking of course. The main herbs I never try to run out of are sage, thyme, basil, star anise, vervain, mint, oregano, cinnamon, coriander and cloves. All these in dried form can quite easily be bought at the local supermarket. But always check the 'Best before' date as even dried herbs can lose their potency.

In many cultures there are remedies that have been passed down through the generations. In Italy it's boiled basil leaves, in Eastern Europe it's chicken soup, for us it's nettle soup. We can get nettle tea in herbal stores and supermarkets now. All of these, boiled basil water, chicken soup and nettle soup are not merely old housewives' tales, they actually do have healing properties in them. We know that chicken soup helps colds and `flu as it not only keeps you hydrated, it is also filled with vitamins and minerals from the vegetables. We also know that basil is an antioxidant and an antiviral, and it can heal an upset stomach. Indeed, I make it into a hard-boiled sweet which is good for a hangover!

As for nettle soup, it is high in minerals including iron and it also has vitamins. Further, it contains histamine which makes it a great natural remedy for hay fever. However, how do we get nettles in the city if we have no garden? Normally you can buy them dried in your local health food shops, though I think it is just a matter of time before we can buy ready-made nettle soup in our supermarkets. If nettle soup does not fill you with joy, try it as a pesto sauce to be used on vegetables or even pasta. The possibilities are endless. Nettles are regarded as a herb and taste a bit like spinach, so basically everything you make with spinach you can do with nettles. If you manage to get hold of fresh ones, always wear gloves and then wash and boil them in water for about three minutes, as this gets the sting out of them; then you are able to make your soups, pesto or whatever. Nettle tea is often made with mint or chamomile, both with their own healing properties. In your Book of Shadows, write down recipes or things you may need or use often. Begin to create your own Book of Shadows with your journey throughout the year.

As we live in the city, there are a number of herbs and remedies that we seem to use often. Commuting to work every day, we are not entirely immune to catching `flu and colds. Therefore, I am going to give you some 'old witch' remedies. Try them and see, use them alongside your usual remedies. But if for example you have a cough lasting longer than a week, check with the doctor (`phone first as you might be contagious).

Prevention is always better than the cure and colds can be prevented by including garlic, onions, watercress and cayenne in your diet. If however you still get colds, here are a couple of remedies.

Ginger Drink
30 g of fresh ginger, sliced
1 stick of cinnamon, broken
1 tsp of coriander seeds
4 cloves
1 slice of lemon, peeled

Simmer all the ingredients in 500 ml of water for 15 minutes, keeping the lid on the pan, then strain and sweeten with honey to taste (Manuka honey is good). Drink a cupful three or four times a day, so brew some up and keep it in a flask to drink throughout the day.

Sore Throat Gargle
30 g sage leaves
3 tsp cider vinegar
1 tsp honey (preferably Manuka)

Make a sage infusion by pouring 500 ml of boiling water onto the sage leaves. Strain this and add the vinegar and honey to the water. Let it cool and then gargle three times a day.

Nose and Sinus Clearing
6 - 8 drops of thyme essential oil
6 - 8 drops of eucalyptus essential oil
3 - 4 drops of peppermint oil

Pour the oils into a mixing bowl with 300 ml of boiling water. Cover your head with a towel and inhale the steam as best you can through your nose until your sinuses feel clearer.

Simple Cough Syrup
Slice a large onion into rings and put them in a deep bowl, then cover them with honey. Cover the bowl either with a tea towel or cling film and leave it overnight. In the morning, strain the mixture to make a cough elixir.

You can also make this in a cleaned jam jar. Slice the onions as before and put a layer of onions in the jar and then a layer of honey, then another layer of onions, then a layer of honey, and so on until it is filled to the top. If you do not like honey you can substitute it with brown sugar. Then put the lid on and leave it overnight; once again, strain the liquid and pour it into a bottle. Keep it in a dark, cool place; it will last for about a week in a refrigerator.

Always label and put the date on anything you make.

Cough Mixture 2
30 g herbal mixture made up from 10 g coltsfoot flowers, 10 g marshmallow leaves, 10 g hyssop
half a liquorice root
half an aniseed

Simmer all the ingredients in 500 ml of water for 15 minutes before straining and adding two teaspoons of honey to the fluid.

Manuka honey is quite expensive but it is very good; however, organic honey is also good and can be used in these remedies. Both cough mixtures can be bottled in an airtight jar and left for no longer than two weeks, after which you should discard what is left; remember, these mixtures have no additives and preservatives in them so they will go off rather quickly.

There are many more spells, potions and concoctions in *Spells in the City*, a whole book dedicated to the art of spellweaving.

If you begin to research further the witches' ways of spells and so forth, you may begin to get confused by the many different terms. For example, if something calls for the 'eye' it is describing the inner part of a plant or flower. Adder's tongue can mean dogtooth, batwing means holly leaves, woodpecker stands for the flower peony, and billings root is good old ginger. Yes, if you begin to look into the old witch books you may find strange names and things you do not understand, things that you may have thought no longer existed. You may be surprised that so many items from the past do still exist, their names simply changed. We witches do change, and that is how we continue to develop and grow by holding onto the past while at the same time developing another way that corresponds to our ever increasingly demanding lives.

However, always remember that we do not hurt any living creature no matter how 'low' on the evolutionary scale. Everything has a place, and let us not forget the most important code, 'An it harm none'.

Enjoy herbs, begin to learn their lore and embrace the healing magic.

Blessed Be

Spells, Incantations & Charms

Dear Reader,

We need to look at some key practices of the witch, such as spells, incantations, charms and enchantment. Some would argue that they are all the same thing but they are subtly not.

The easiest to understand is the spell. A spell is 'a command to the universe', whatever you deem that to be, for something to happen. Further, spell-making is a form of spell-weaving, as the universe has many intricate components within it which we use to spin magic on. Spells are collections of words or commands. We start by describing the problem and how we want it to be resolved magically, and then the spell is closed by 'So mote it be'. Many spells have a rhyming tone to them, because this adds a rhythm to it which holds power. The more you say and repeat it the stronger the spell - you are enforcing your will onto something. That is why it is so important that you act with responsibility.

Let us create a money spell, for example a spell at the end of the month. Taking the first step, the problem is that I have no money at the end of the month. What is the desired outcome? I want some money at the end of the month. So this becomes:

At the end of the month, money I have none.
At the end of this month, I would like some.

I can of course change 'month' to 'week' if needs be, as I may really need the money. I am also not putting a figure on how much money I want because I am allowing the universe to give me what I really need to get by until the end of the month or until I get paid again. I make my command specific; however, I also want to show that for my part I am honest and am acting responsibly. Thus:

> *At the end of the month, money I have none.*
> *At the end of this week, I would like some*
> *So that I may pay bills and have what I need.*
> *To the universe I show no greed.*

I now need to show that it is finished and it will harm no-one. Spells have a way of turning out in a certain way, so we always put in a clause that no-one will be harmed or hurt by our command. So our spell complete is:

> *At the end of the month, money I have none.*
> *At the end of this week, I would like some*
> *So that I may pay bills and have what I need.*
> *To the universe I show no greed.*
> *An it harm none, so mote it be.*

Now, we have made a spell and we could just repeat it, but let us do some weaving, using threads within the universe. Green is the colour of money, so let us light a green candle while we recite the spell. The day is important too, and Friday is a good day to begin this on. We need to recite this spell every night for a week, from Friday to Friday, while lighting the green candle and reciting our spell. Now try writing a spell of your own and always make sure that you write any spells in your BOS, your Book of Shadows.

The next piece of magical work we need to look at is the charm. A charm is not a spell, not a command to the universe to do something. Rather, it is like a wish placed onto something or someone. There is not necessarily a specific outcome with a charm, and there is not a beginning, middle and end. Charms never usually come to an end and when we charm something it is forever or for as long as we are alive.

A charm can be either for good or bad, and a bad charm is called a hex. We never hex. I know it might be so tempting but really we do not do that - ever! A charm is usually a blessing placed onto someone or something for good. You are charming something for the benefit of others. Think of the words that spring to mind when you think of 'charm': lucky, gifted, hope and magic.

Let us charm a necklace for love. Find a necklace, perhaps with a heart shape. Hold it in your hands and say, "Blessings upon this necklace. Whoever finds it will always find true love. Blessed Be." When we imprint the goodwill onto the heart necklace, it is now a charm. Many people have a 'lucky' charm, something that they believe brings them good fortune. The common charms are four-leaf clovers, talismans or amulets that may have been blessed by someone, or by you yourself. You can create your own good luck charm just by instilling a positive vibration onto the object.

An enchantment is something similar. Think of the word 'enchanting' and look to nature; what does the cobra do? It enchants its prey by its dance. It is an alluring, captivating, bewitching dance, of course inevitably ending with eating the prey. The world of nature is fierce and is to be respected. If something is enchanted it becomes alluring and fascinating. Think of fairy tales such as Cinderella and the glass slippers. The slippers were enchanted but it was Cinderella who captivated and enchanted the Prince. Enchantments can be upon people just as in nature, whereas charms are usually upon objects and places. The snow stick that I shall discuss later is a charm; it has an enchantment upon it but it itself is a charm. The enchantment does not need to be said again, like a spell; it has already been infused with the power required to be used forever as a charm.

An incantation is a series of words, usually formulaic and similar to a spell but not quite a command. It is usually a request or an invocation, a chant as it were, to create whatever is desired. However, we would not use an incantation for money - we would use a spell. Rather, we might use an incantation to create good luck for a team or for an endeavour, either for an individual or for a group. An incantation is also a request to the god or goddess we follow. This is a powerful request and one that is not to be taken lightly. The bell is an object often used with an incantation to create an extra boost.

The power of an incantation is not to be misunderstood. In terms of focusing one's power, a spell would come first, then an incantation, followed by a charm, then an enchantment.

I hope the differences have been made clear, dear reader, and you find your way through the maze of ancient spells and incantations. Please always use caution, remember the Rede and be careful with what you are invoking.

Blessed Be

Familiars

Dear Reader,

You may be aware of this term. But if not, a familiar is an animal who finds his or her way to you as your guide from nature. A familiar can be anything from a cat to a dog, a rabbit, horse or snake, a crow or even a salamander... I know! This gift from nature can take many forms but the animal will always find you - the cat that is always at your door, or the robin that is always around you. A friend of mine had a salamander living by the front door who wanted to come in. My own familiar is a crow; wherever I have been in the world there has been a crow, cawing at my window from Italy to California.

These familiar gifts come as guides, as a spiritual connection to the Earth, a reminder of who we are; they are also an indication of our strength as every animal represents an element that we are stronger working with. A cat represents psychic abilities - the crystal ball, the Tarot, and work with spirit and ultimately the goddess. A dog is for healing, so work with crystals and especially animal healing; also, all dogs are sacred to Hecate. The salamander is associated with psychic ability and transformation; it represents dreams and their meanings and scrying. The crow is all about mystery and pure magic, so any form of spell-casting and alchemy are represented with the appearance of this beautiful bird. Familiars are also regarded as being naturally attuned to seasons and phases of the moon.

The familiar will makes its presence known to you, but you must be aware of it so always look out for the signs. Once you begin to embrace the Craft and acknowledge the fact you are a witch, these signs will become apparent to you; please do not dismiss them for they are gifts to you.

You can get many books about animal signs and their meanings from good bookstores, but here is a list of the most common animals that, being a witch, you may come into contact with as gifts from nature. Remember that the familiar is both your guide and your strength. You may be an all-round witch but the appearance of a familiar in your life is telling you that you need to concentrate on a particular aspect of the Craft.

- **Cat** — Confidence, psychic ability; the goddess Bast. (White cats – Freya)
- **Dog** — Friendship, healing; Hecate.
- **Rabbit** — Opportunity; Ostara/Eostre.
- **Horse** — Strength; Epona.
- **Snake** — Power; Lilith.
- **Owl** — Wisdom; Athena.
- **Lizard** — Change; Luna.
- **Butterfly** — Freedom; Psyche.
- **Dove** — Peace; Aphrodite.
- **Crow** — Magic; Morrigan.

Further, when you start seeing this animal every day and all around you, you may realise that you have always seen it; the chances are that this animal familiar has always been with you in some form. As I have said, once born a witch, always a witch. Your familiar has walked beside you since birth. Remember, it could be anything from a particular type of bird to a particular type of insect. On the other hand, you may not have a familiar animal that has always been with you or you constantly see, and that's fine. It may mean that you do not need a familiar, and not every witch has one.

Look out for the signs, write them in your BOS, and allow yourself to be surprised.

Blessed Be

Warlocks, Broomsticks, Scrying ~ Oh My!

Dear Reader,

Here I would like to dispel some myths that have grown up around being a witch. One of them in particular is that of a 'warlock'. Just for the record, a warlock is not a male witch. A male witch is a male witch, or a wizard if they so wish to be called, or simply a practitioner of the Craft. Warlock means an oath breaker or liar. There are legends surrounding warlocks and they usually pertain to someone who practises 'the dark arts'. A witch is a witch and it does not matter what gender the person is. During the dark days of history, both men and women were tried as witches and those who were found guilty of practising witchcraft were killed, male and female alike.

Another word that seems to pop up along the way is the term 'scrying'. Other terms for scrying are seeing or peeping and that is exactly what it means. It is a practice used for divination and fortune telling. There are several ways we can scry; of course, crystal balls are one method but others include using stones, glass, cards, mirrors, water, fire and smoke. Mirrors are a particularly good method and many witches have a special scrying mirror that is normally wrapped up and kept out of plain view. We scry in order to see things past, present and future.

One of the main scrying activities that is very common has now turned into a spell. It is usually performed on Hallowe'en:

> *On Hallowe'en look in the mirrored glass*
> *and your future husband shall surely pass.*

One of the most famous scryers was Nostradamus who used the bowl of water technique to see the future and write his quatrains. Others choose to look into the flames of a candle to see the future. Further, some may scry with a pendulum, usually a crystal on a long piece of leather, ribbon or cord. There will be two cards with the words Yes or No written on them. Basically, you ask your question and hold the pendulum above the words to see which way it swings.

Another sort of myth surrounding witches is the practice of being skyclad. The term means that a witch practises her or his spells, ceremonies and rituals naked. The term skyclad is actually quite a modern term and only became known and used in the last century. Its origins, some believe, were in India and some religious traditions associated with naked practice. 'Digambara' literally means 'sky-clothes'. So it is not too far a stretch of the imagination that this term and the practices involved found their way into our culture and history.

It is one of those aspects of being a witch that is entirely personal and up to you. Some people may feel uncomfortable with this and that is fine, while others do not. My only advice is not to do it in a public park as you will probably be arrested!

So from being completely naked let us look into the robe. Robes are entirely up to the witch herself or himself. Some witches prefer the iconic black robes that reach to the ground because they suggest wisdom. Green is another colour that is worn because it represents the spring. Red has also been used at times, usually for Beltane or the summer solstice, while others have been known to wear long white robes that represent purity. However all forms of fastenings, such as buttons or buckles, are avoided except for loose usually cord belts.

But there really is no set dress that you have to wear to perform a ritual, ceremony or spell; jeans and tee-shirts are fine. It is what's inside that matters, the intent and the love stemming from the heart that are important. Wear whatever you feel comfortable in and if that is skyclad or in a robe, then fine. Remember, there is no doctrine, no right or wrong, except that you always act with responsibility.

Black cats are regarded in some communities as evil and bad luck. However, in Britain the black cat symbolises magic without malevolence and is considered very lucky. To have one cross your path is a sign of auspicious times ahead. Yet there is all sorts of lore regarding whether it crosses your path from left to right, or if the cat runs away it is generally regarded as bad luck. Further, if a black cat visits your home you should not chase it away as it will take the good luck with it. Anyway, it may also be your familiar and a gift from the goddess Bast.

But why are black cats associated with witches and witchcraft? Well, the chances are that in many of the witch trials the accused would say after a few days of torture that their familiar was a cat, or the devil was their familiar, or the devil appeared to them in the form of a black cat. Crows and of course frogs were also popular as familiars and the devil's imps. However, we must take these accounts with a pinch of salt (preferably magic salt). But seriously, many of the traditions and superstitions we have today are owed to those dark times. The witch trials were the beginnings of today's clichés.

If you want a black cat, go ahead and embrace the cliché. I am of the view that all animals are blessed and deserve a good home; there are no curses on any animal, there are no evil animals, and all deserve respect and care from us. Incidentally, in pet rescue and cats' protection centres they have more black cats available than any other kind of animal or cat. They are always the last to be adopted merely because of superstition! So do not be put off by superstition; you are a witch, you are powerful and there is nothing you cannot deal with. Do not be scared away by the colour of an animal. Blessed Be to you for looking after the animals and especially black cats.

We might as well discuss the conical hat here too. The traditional witch's hat was probably adopted because of the magical shape, the cone of power or the typical pyramid shape which symbolises and focuses energy and power. Conical or pointy hats have been worn since the beginning of civilisation, from Europe through to Japan and India. In fact, there are images and depictions of Odysseus wearing them in ancient Greece, where they were known as pilos.

So the witches' hats that are sold to children for Hallowe'en, so they can be witches and wizards, are not a cliché but a really important ceremonial piece of history that connects us to the past. Nowadays we may have a pointy hat for a joke but witches do not wear them - or maybe some do? Blessed Be to my sisters and brothers of the past, present and future who still wear the pointy hat!

Now the broomstick - the word we use for this is the besom. It is used in magic to cleanse and purify an area of negativity. It is usually made from straw although it can be made with any leafy twigs, and is especially nice if made with dried herbs, in particular lavender. A small lavender besom made with a twig of willow and tied with a ribbon is a beautiful present to give anyone. I have a small one about 15 cm long with a red ribbon and a little bell tied to it. It is purely for remembrance and observance of ancestors who have passed. A besom also acts as a guard to the house and mine is placed up above the door. Some witches still use their besom in rituals. They sweep the area prior to a ritual clockwise, usually from east to west, following the path of the sun.

So there you have it, some myths hopefully quashed about warlocks, going skyclad and black cats. These are untruths and clichés, while broomsticks, pointy hats, scrying and robes are to an extent real.

Blessed Be

The Witch Trials

Dear Reader,

No book about witches would be complete without some explanation or description of the dark days in our past. The witch trials were in every part of Christendom and that should be a huge clue to some of the reasons for them. The world was going through constant change from Reformation to revolution, from scientific breakthroughs to new worlds being discovered. The new worlds themselves had their own form of witchcraft, with witch doctors, medicine men, healers and shamans. Magic finds a way to all the purest of hearts and it survives in whatever form it can.

Yet returning to Europe and in particular the United Kingdom, in nearly every county there is a story of a witch; not all of them resulted in torture and death though a great many did. There were many trials and the most famous ones are of the Pendle Hill witches, the St Osyth witches which included Ursula Kemp, and the witches of Berwick who, it is alleged, tried to kill King James by conjuring up a storm at sea when the king was returning home with his new bride.

However, there are other lesser known cases such as the witches of Belvoir, a mother and her two daughters who were accused of stealing when they worked for the Earl and Countess of Rutland at Belvoir Castle near Grantham in Lincolnshire. The son of the Earl and Countess was taken ill and died, so of course the women were blamed and accused of witchcraft. The mother died in jail while her two daughters were hanged. In Lincolnshire there is the tale of the Revesby witches, and the strange tree that looks like a witch flying on her broomstick. As legend would have it, there is a witch buried underneath that very tree. Even in the city of London the past calls to us and we walk in the footsteps of our sisters and brothers of the Craft. In 2004 a 'witches' bottle' was dug up in Greenwich. These bottles were very popular in the 16th and 17th centuries. Legends and stories abound here in the United Kingdom and the rest of the world about witches and what they got up to.

Yet the witchcraft trials are not just in the distant past, the most recent being in 1944. Helen Duncan was a Spiritualist who told parents that their son had been killed in a naval battle that no-one had heard of at the time. She was convicted under the Witchcraft Act of 1735 and spent nine months in Holloway Prison.

The fear and prejudice surrounding witches still prevails today but hopefully not as ferociously as it did in the past. In my tradition we have a special day of remembrance for the fallen and for all those wrongly accused of witchcraft, on the 30th October. The 29th of October is the day of Hecate, goddess of magic and therefore of witches. The 30th is the day of remembrance and the 31st is Hallowe'en, a new year's day, a new spiritual Turning of the Wheel. That is why in our house Samhain lasts longer than just one night for us. We light candles of blue and white for the fallen and say a special blessing:

> *Blessed spirits of sisters and brothers past,*
> *Whose lives cruelly suffered with lies,*
> *Find peace, serenity and love at last.*
> *No more the bitter tortured cries.*
> *Thank you for the lessons of your lives.*
> *Rejoice now among the Summerlands and stars.*
> *May your souls soar free and far.*
> *Blessed Be to one and all.*

In Scotland over 1,500 people have been executed as witches, while in England Mathew Hopkins, the Witch Finder General, is thought to have executed 200 - 400 witches alone. The real figure of how many were burned in Britain could be anywhere from several hundred to thousands during the dark times. Yet those who fell during the dark days are acknowledged.

But we continue to learn and grow. Remember always to act responsibly and be careful whom you tell about your beliefs.

Blessed Be

Reincarnation

Dear Reader,

As this book is about being a witch in the city and the fundamental practices, rituals and tools needed in order for you to begin your path as a witch, I want to try to answer some important questions you may have. There are things you may be wondering about, things you cannot seem to understand such as why you do not like a particular thing or why you are drawn to a particular place or time.

In the Festivals of Life letter we mentioned where a witch goes when he or she leaves the mortal plane - the Summerlands. We do believe in reincarnation; recycling is nothing new, dear Reader! Is there a particular part of history that you are drawn to? I don't mean just a particular era you like studying but a feeling much more powerful. It is as if when you look at that page of history you can sense it, you smell the smells of that time and you hear the people of that time. You can see yourself in the market or walking down the streets of that time. That era in history is as alive for you as today is. It is not just a black and white page in history, it is real and you are a part of it.

If you sense and feel these things of one particular era then it is highly likely that you are remembering your past. The times that are alive for me are Roman, Viking, Imperial Russian and the First World War. So alive are the memories that thinking of these times triggers powerful emotions in me. The First World War especially is very traumatic. You may have similar experiences and do not know why. It is highly likely that when you step upon the path of a witch, you will feel you have come home, as it were, and you will sense these things more. Being a witch is as much about the spiritual as it is about the practical - the casting of spells, making potions and sending healing.

If you do have these feelings then do not run away from them, read up on that time and learn to embrace your past lives, all of them, and try to heal the pain that was felt and remember the happiness.

One of the key feelings for many people that I have come across is the fear of having anything around their neck. This could be an indication that they were hung in a past life as a witch. Further, it could also signify a death by guillotine or decapitation by the axe man here in England.

The most common methods of execution for witches were hanging, drowning and burning. Here in Europe, burning was the most popular as not only was it considered the most painful, also one of the most effective ways to exorcise the devil was by fire - sending him back to the flames of hell. The American colonies, however, favoured hanging in cases of witchcraft and the United Kingdom had its fair share of hangings too. Although it is not possible to know for certain how many men, women and children were executed for witchcraft throughout the world, scholars estimate it to be around forty to fifty thousand people.

As the saying goes, once a witch always a witch. If you do dislike anything around your neck like a necklace, scarf even a turtleneck jumper, then welcome home! Blessed Be, sister or brother, you are most welcome and very much needed in the world at this time.

Blessed Be

Coven or Solitary Witch?

Dear Reader,

We now come to the paths of the witch and which one you will go down.

A coven is a group that is made up usually of anything between seven and thirteen members. However, even a group of three people could also be called a coven. The term itself was a medieval word meaning a gathering of any kind. The witch trials of the 1600s made it a popular term to describe a group of witches, so traditionally a coven has had that meaning. However, it seems that in the 21st century the word is now used to describe a group of vampires… As I say, things change!

A coven will meet on a regular basis to acknowledge the movements of the moon, celebrate the sabbats and the festivals of the year. There will usually be a High Priestess and perhaps a High Priest too; if so, the coven will be jointly led by both. The coven will initiate people, complete spells and perform rituals such as Hand Fasting and Wiccaning within their group. Some people like to be in a coven for 'safety in numbers', they say!

However, there is nothing written anywhere saying that those who practise witchcraft have to be in a coven. Indeed, if anything the Craft is an individualistic religion; you are after all responsible for your own actions even in a coven. Having an elder or powerful High Priestess on your side when things get rough can be a wonderful feeling, a great bonus throughout this life, and it is also good to have someone to ask about a spell and check if it is right.

Yet still I come back to the point that the Craft is individualistic. You may make mistakes with spells, but as long as you live by the Rede, 'an it harm none', then nothing catastrophic should come back to you. We learn by our mistakes, we learn through experience. A solitary practitioner is sometimes known as a hedge witch. She or he does all their spells, rituals and ceremonies on their own. They need no-one else in order to live as a witch. They live by the Rede and generally keep themselves to themselves.

If however you would still prefer to be in a coven, there are a number of ways to do this. There are now witch covens on the Internet. There are advertisements in magazines for groups, or you could put your own advertisement in any of the spiritual magazines for likeminded people to contact you. You never know, there might be several people in your area who would like to be in a coven too. There are also festivals held, pagan and Wiccan ones, so look out for these and see if you can get to one. There are many groups to be found at festivals that may be interesting for you.

However, I would add, please always be careful when approaching groups, either in person or online; be respectful and only talk to those whom you feel you can trust.

Blessed Be

Initiation

Dear Reader,

We have now reached the moment of initiation. This is something that is very personal and purely up to you. It is not to be taken lightly, as those who become witches will always remain witches, and it is a path of great responsibility. After all, it is essentially a religion, a belief system where you are in control of it yourself. The only creed is the Wiccan Rede, 'an it harm none'. That is a lot of responsibility and a lot of power in your hands. I say again, please act responsibly.

So, if you have lived at least a year as a witch, you have followed our ways and you are absolutely sure that this is what you want, then let us begin. If you have come to the realisation you do not want to be in a coven, then your initiation must be a self-initiation. There are many books written about this but here I will describe my tradition.

I know I have said that going skyclad is a matter of choice, but this is the one time when you really do need to be naked. Make sure you have the house or apartment to yourself, so you will be on your own and there will be no-one to disturb you. You will be naked because you should think of it as being born into a new life.

The Initiation Ceremony

Make a circle using your salt or salt water, and as you do so say:

I caste the circle, this circle I summon.
I ask only positive energies to enter here.
I work for the light and the good.
Salt, banish the negativity,
Disperse any entities that would do me harm.
Blessed Be.
So mote it be.

In the circle there should be placed a dish of sea salt, a yellow candle representing air, a red one for fire, a green one for earth and a blue one of course for water. Some may say that you need them in the north, south, east and west corners of your circle but many of us do not have the space or a compass. There's no need to run around the house looking for the right spiritual focus centre. This is your initiation and no-one else's, so keep to the basics; remember, you are creating this now.

Also in your circle you will have some jasmine oil for anointing yourself. (I also had an oil burner with the oils sweet magnolia and vanilla in it.) The place needs to be calm and tranquil as you try to centre yourself. If you have an image of the Green Man and an image of a goddess, then put these in your circle too as they will help you to focus your concentration. There will also be the pentagram; you could have an apple sliced in half to reveal the pentagram, or you could have drawn a special one.

You should have written out beforehand your vows to the Goddess and God, but if not then just speak from the heart for this is in a sense your wedding day, your union with the divine. You will pledge your allegiance to the divine, to protect and defend nature in all her forms. You will promise not to impose your will on any living thing. You will ask the Goddess and God if they will accept you as a witch.

> *Now speak your vows.*

At this, the candles may flicker or they may be a small noise or something that takes your attention; do not worry and do not break the circle. If there isn't anything like this, that's fine too. I am just preparing you that anything might happen, but it is above all a lesson of acceptance.

As you speak your vows to the Goddess and God, you dab the centre of your brow and also your wand, the index finger, with the jasmine oil. Finish your vows by saying:

> *I am consecrated in the names of*
> *the Great Mother and the Great God.*

Sit for some time thinking about your new life. Then when you feel you are ready you can close the circle by thanking the air, fire, water and earth for witnessing your initiation to the Craft, then blow out the candles. Thank the Goddess and the God and finish by saying:

> *Blessed Be to one and all.*
> *So mote it be.*

That is it, your initiation is over, and all there is left to say is "Welcome to the club!"

Blessed Be

What Kind of Witch?

Dear Reader,

While writing this book I came to realise that the Craft is developing as we also develop. My ancestors would be amazed and probably shake their heads in denial at the changes that some people have brought about, but my ancestors are not of this time. The Craft grows and expands as does our knowledge. In our world we seem to categorise everything, to the extent that there are now several types of witch, not just one but rather a number of classifications or categories of witches.

As science grows alongside us, our knowledge of the Craft develops further. Scientific breakthroughs enhance our knowledge of herbs, crystals and geology. So one can begin to understand the need to categorise witches by certain criteria. At present there are roughly six types: Earth witch, hedge witch, Gardnerian, Dianic, eclectic and kitchen witches.

An Earth witch is precisely what you would think it means, someone who works very closely with the Earth. So their specialisms, as it were, would be working with animals and with crystals, recognising the changing seasons, blessing plants, and using herb lore, plants and their medicinal properties. The Earth witch might be in a coven or practising Earth lore by themselves.

A hedge witch is a solitary practitioner of the Craft who does everything, covering every aspect of the Craft and working on their own. They do not need to belong to a coven or any set order to practise the Craft. They may do healing, spells, practise herb lore, work with animals, and acknowledge the Turning of the Wheel.

The kitchen witch is exactly what it sounds like it should be, someone who is always brewing potions and concoctions for spells. He or she is someone who prefers to be in the kitchen quite literally baking, or making something usually magical in origin. Once again they can be either in a coven or preferring a solitary mode of practice. They too would acknowledge the changing seasons and the festivals of the changing wheel of the year.

However, you will notice that I have put these three types together because basically they are the same. For me, a witch is a witch! Moreover, as for the eclectic witch, well, that's a bit of everything as the name implies. If you follow the code, the Rede, no matter how you follow it you are still a witch. You might have a preference to work with animals and crystals and nothing else. But ask yourself this, do you write spells or make spells to help the animals heal? Do you work with crystals because you believe in their healing power? Do you believe in magic? If so then you are a witch regardless of any preference you have. You are just a witch who prefers to be in a kitchen, or outdoors, or on their own, or with a group of like-minded friends.

Yet there are also different strands of the belief system within the Craft and one of them is Gardnerian. Gerald Gardner is the founder of the tradition that is named after him, and some argue that he is the founder of 'modern witchcraft'. Gardner learned his beliefs and traditions from the New Forest Coven in the 1930s and 1940s. The term Wicca was also reused by him and now Gardnerian, Alexandrian and Algard Wicca are regarded as original traditions of what is termed British Traditional Wicca. Membership of British Traditional Wicca is generally only through initiation within a group by a High Priestess or High Priest. These groups usually have thirteen members, though they can have less or more. They celebrate and acknowledge both the God and Goddess.

Another significant type of witchcraft in the world today is called Dianic Witchcraft, or Feminist Witchcraft. Founded in the USA during the 1970s it combines many elements we have already discussed, such as British Traditional Wicca, alongside folk magic and feminist values. It has predominantly all-female covens. They worship the Goddess and follow the eight major festivals of the year.

There are now many more categories popping up here and there, re-defining the belief system. As one who is a hereditary witch, I would have to agree with my ancestors somewhat. A witch is a witch. Follow the code, help the Earth and your fellow people as best you can, honour the Goddess and the God, be true to yourself and always believe in magic, then you are a witch!

There are always different traditions of witchcraft and normally these come from other countries. The African witchcraft traditions are very different to ours, which in turn are different to the Asian or oriental forms of witchcraft. Each of these traditions has in themselves differences, from voodoo to hoodoo to Lilitu. In some forms of African witchcraft, for example, the sacrifice of animals is paramount for a spell or incantation to work. While with other animal sacrificial forms of witchcraft the animal is killed quickly and painlessly, in some African forms, especially, if the animal screams loudly then the spirits of the ancestors can hear it and will help with the spell and invocation. In our tradition this is something completely alien to us, but it is another people's version of the Craft and one that is many thousands of years old.

Another form of witchcraft that many people seem to adhere to, and take pieces of information and practices from, is that of American Nativism. Native American witchcraft has many characteristics that are similar to ours; one in particular is the use of amulets and charms, but this is true of many witchcrafts. These people lived completely off the land and many herbs and rituals for the healing of mind, body and soul really stem from what the American settlers encountered. The sweat lodge and its benefits for the mind are well known indeed, another term for it being a medicine house or medicine lodge.

Further, the use of crystals within Native American witchcraft was also crucial in the diagnosis and healing of the sick. The shamans were of either sex but were predominately women; the medicine woman of the village would perform rites and rituals for the healing of the sick with herbs. She would perform rituals for the weather or to ensure a good harvest. The rain stick is another tool that seems to have come our way, though generally we do not need it in our country! Rain sticks originally stem from the South American Indians of Peru and Chile. They were made from cactus which is hollow and dried out in the sun, then filled with small pebbles or beans, though not completely as the beans or pebbles need to be able to run up and down the stick sounding like rain.

As we have little need of rain sticks in England, but snow is something that is rather hit and miss with us, I have created an alternative called the snow stick. Instead of beans or pebbles I use salt in a small tube sealed at both ends, painted white and decorated with images of snow. The salt, when it is falling down the tube, is soft and light like snow. I have put an enchantment on the snow stick too:

> *Blessed stick of ancestors passed,*
> *Grant falling salt in this stick turn to snow.*
> *Snow please, grant for fun and not woe.*
> *Blessed Be an it harm none.*
> *Snow, snow, snow, snow.*

The varying forms of witchcraft that prevail today can be seen in all corners of the world. Here in the west we have developed our own in relation to our environment, as have other lands. When we look at other forms of the Craft we view them as sister or brother traditions. We view them with respect and we learn from each other. There are so many other forms of witch that are sprouting up throughout the world; they are even named after the colours of the rainbow.

But perhaps this is going too far. Soon we will lose a clear definition of what a witch is, if we are not careful. Look at Christianity: how many variants are there in that religion and yet they all come under the category of Christian? That is precisely what witchcraft is like; there are many differing kinds but we are really all the same… we all believe in magic!

> *So Blessed Be to one and all,*
> *Our different paths bring us to the same,*
> *Our love of magic and belief.*
> *We all reside under one name.*
> *So mote it be.*

Blessed Be

A Witch's Dictionary

Dear Reader,

We have now come to the end of this book and I hope you have enjoyed it. However, it is not quite the end as I have put a dictionary of some of our weird and wonderful phrases and terms in the next few pages.

So much of our past can disappear in the light of new discoveries and technologies so I have put together some of my favourite sayings and phrases from ancestors' recipe books. One of my favourites would have to be 'Elf Shot'. It has nothing to do with Santa's little helpers becoming a gun-wielding gang, though inevitably it is the witches who are behind this delightful term!

This book set out to dispel some of the myths and clichés regarding being a witch. We have also looked at the dark days, the changing times, and the differences between certain groups within witchcraft. Hopefully, you now realise what you are and have become initiated and therefore are now a part of the gang! It is a wonderful life, though also one of great responsibility.

There is so much more to learn and to understand, and we have merely scratched the surface. To be a witch is to be a part of the greater universe, yet you are also an individual. We are both a part of the collective and also completely responsible for our own lives. Our choices determine our actions which can impinge on others, so always act with love and caution.

Blessed Be

There are so many words and phrases that modern witches may not know or be aware of. So I have devised this dictionary of some of the really obscure terms and beliefs that may have been forgotten in time.

A word of warning, though. There are some herbs here that can be used for medicinal purposes but you should always check their properties with a physician and if in doubt DO NOT use them. Always act responsibly!

Enjoy and Blessed Be.

Adder's Mouth
This has many names such as Bog Orchid, Bog Adder's Mouth, Green Adder's Mouth or White Adder's Mouth. It is a small, single-leafed orchid, used in herbalism to treat wounds and bruises.

Adder Stones
These are naturally occurring glassy stones with a hole through them. They are also called Serpent's Eggs, Druid's Glass and Wizard's Glass. They can come in many colours such as green, pink, red, blue and brown and are sacred to druids.

Adder's Tongue
This is a plant that is also known as Dogtooth Violet, Fawn Lily or Trout Lily. The bulb is edible as a root vegetable and can also be ground into flour. It has been used as an emetic and as a poultice applied to tumours and ulcers.

Angelica
A large flowering plant with a pleasant perfume, valued for its flavour in liqueurs and as a remedy for colds and rheumatism. More importantly, as the name implies, it attract angels and banish demons.

Amulet
There are so many amulets and every culture, time and people has at least one that is significant to them. An amulet is a talisman, an object that is given great power either to ward off evil or to protect the wearer or the house.

Blocula
A site in Sweden which was a large meadow where the Mora witches went to perform their rituals. This particular case of witch hysteria and the subsequent trials is an excellent example of mass hysteria to study, as over 300 children were involved; it also managed to engulf Finland.

Brocken
One of the most famous places in Germany for the sabbat of Walpurgis Night on April 30th.

Buying Wind
What a lovely term for Storm Raising and, yes, witches are alleged to be responsible for making storms. So Buying Wind, of course, is witches making deals with the devil to raise a storm that will destroy harvests, crops, houses or even kings at sea!

Captoptromancy
This is another term for scrying.

Charm Wand
I love this one - it is a glass stick, almost as big as a walking stick, which is filled with beads or seeds. It guards the house and it is said that a demon could not resist counting the seeds which of course stops them from committing any crimes against the occupant of the house.

Chimney
Apparently witches in a coven would often depart after a ritual on their broomsticks up the chimney - a Wiccan alternative to Santa perhaps!

Conjuration
The same as divination.

Dragon's Blood
Sorry, not really the blood of dragons but actually a plant that is native to the Canary Islands. It has been used for millennia, since the times of the Romans and ancient Greeks, for healing wounds and for gastrointestinal and respiratory conditions. Nowadays it is popular for skin rejuvenation.

Elf Shot
An unexpected decline in the health of someone in the local village, said of course to be the work of witches, or fairies under the guidance of a witch. In other words, it is a witch's curse.

Esbat
A monthly gathering at the full moon, which can be indoors or outdoors. It is a time when we can perform assistance to those who are ill or in trouble; but normally there are only three spells at any Esbat, as our energy would wane otherwise.

Five Fold Kiss
Not a really passionate kiss, but actually a kiss by the High Priest during the Dance of the Wheel, which celebrates the winter solstice.

Garlic
It is not only good for getting rid of vampires but a brilliant all-round herb for everything from protection to dental hygiene. It has been used all over the world from ancient Egypt to the modern world.

Hand of Glory
Or should it be Hand of Gory, as it is the severed hand of a hanged man. Apparently, a hand of glory was very popular in medieval witchcraft beliefs of the British Isles.

Hag stone
A stone or pebble with a hole in it. It is a bit like 'the evil eye' or the Hand of Fatima, as it is an amulet that wards off evil.

Iron
Iron is forged in fire and is considered the most magical of all metals. It is allegedly a deterrent against witches, dragons and ghosts - the usual offenders!

Jimson Weed
This is a highly poisonous plant that can kill, found in the Americas. It is a hallucinogen but has also been used as an analgesic and to relieve asthma. It has other names such as thorn apple, stinkweed, Jimpson Weed and Devil's Weed.

Kudin Tree
The leaves of this rare tropical tree are used as a tea in Chinese herbal medicine. It is apparently beneficial for the heart, brain and stomach.

Logan Stone
A big boulder that is positioned so that it can rock forwards and backwards. There is a lovely legend from Cornwall that says touching a Logan stone nine times at midnight would instantly transform you into a witch… no, I haven't tried it!

Mandrake
This is one of those herbs that is always mentioned with regard to witches. It has been used since the beginning of time as an aphrodisiac and a major contribution in sex magic. So much so that in England we called it love apples, though in past centuries the fruit was also called the devil's apples. But take care – when the root is dug up it is said to scream, killing all who hear it!

Mirrors
There are many superstitions. Many of the ancients believed that when a person looked into a mirror their soul would move into the reflection. In Victorian times, a broken mirror was said to mean the death of a family member or friend. Mirrors are often used in scrying and meditation.

Nightshade
We call it 'deadly nightshade' and it is precisely that. The berries of this herbaceous shrub contain belladonna which is a hallucinogen and can also be highly toxic. In certain preparations, however, it has many medicinal uses such as pain relief and as an anti-inflammatory. Belladonna was one of the key components in the witch's 'flying' potion of yesteryear.

Oak
This tree is sacred to all but we have many superstitions regarding it. They are extraordinary, such as hammering a nail into the poor tree to relieve you of toothache. People also believed that the oak tree could ward off evil spirits, so much so that some people would wear oak leaves while others would keep acorns in the house to ward off lightning. Further, fairies are said to live in oak trees.

Periwinkle Powder
Sprinkle some under your bed and enjoy! Yes, it's one of those herbs.

Poppet
A poppet is an image of someone, like a doll, but it is used in spells, sometimes for healing though also associated with putting curses on someone by sticking pins in the effigy.

Qetesh

A goddess of pleasure! She originally stems from Sumeria but was also worshipped by the Egyptians as an aspect of Hathor. She is a deity of pure pleasure, including sexual. Snakes are her animal, of course, and another symbol is the crescent moon.

Rosemary

One of the key herbs you need in your cupboard; not only good for flavouring food, it is also an excellent herb for love enchantments and can be used in spells provoking lust.

Samson Root

A purple coneflower, the root was used to treat stings and snake bites. It is a component of Echinacea, said to strengthen the immune system. But it also increases virility, allegedly, so carry some in your pocket.

Silver

It is regarded as one of the most pure and potent of all metals. Apart from the killing of werewolves, it is also good for getting rid of witches as normal bullets can be warded off by spells while silver cannot be corrupted by magic.

Sow Thistle

Also known as hare thistle, this is a common weed surprisingly rich in vitamins and minerals, used in herbal medicine to treat liver and kidney ailments among others. It can also be helpful in invisibility spells. No, haven't tried that either!

Stonecrop

This one is quite self-explanatory; it is a flower that grows on the side of rocks and or walls. In the past it has been used to treat epilepsy and skin diseases. But please remember always to consult a physician before treating any ailment with herbs.

Toadflax
A weed, also known as Devil's Ribbon, which has been used in herbal medicine as an astringent and diuretic. A very good plant for breaking hexes too.

Transvection
The ability of witches to fly through the air on broomsticks. Many now believe that this image is due to the use of psychoactive substances... but we know what we choose to believe, don't we?

Undine
An undine is a sea fairy of Greece, not to be confused with mermaids. But she is definitely a mystical creature of the sea whose name actually means wave.

Vinegar
This is actually a great component to have in all manner of healing potions. It is better tolerated and more in keeping with the pH level of the skin. Therefore it is useful for the skin, in washes, and also for hair preparations. Moreover, vinegar can be diluted with warm water and used for sprains and bruises, while diluted with cold or iced water it becomes an excellent compress for tension headaches or hot swollen joints.

Widdershins
This means anti-clockwise, or steering something in the opposite direction.

Willow
These trees are said to uproot themselves and follow you through the woods at night. You have been warned.

X
On the Gardnerian pentacle there are three X-shaped crosses that represent those anointing in an initiation ceremony.

Youth

The Celtic deity of youth was also the deity of healing, water, beauty, writing and magic among other things. He was known by many titles such as the Cloud Maker, Silver Hand and, my favourite, He Who Bestows Wealth. His name is Nuada.

Zodiac

I could have started this witch's alphabet with astrology but instead I now end it with zodiac. Every country has a zodiac of some kind. Here in the west we have 12 signs of the zodiac: 3 water signs, 3 earth signs, 3 air signs and 3 fire signs - the elements get everywhere! However, there is also Chinese astrology with their animal signs, while in India they have Vedic astrology. Research them all and have fun looking into them. Remember, witches like to know about everything, so listen and learn.

To Come in this Series

Spells in the City
One hundred spells for the modern practitioner of the Craft, covering everything you would need: spells for different occasions and festivals, focusing on the art of correspondences.

Magic in the City
The different forms of magic in the city, focusing on English and Celtic magic, and looking at the different practices and traditions. Also includes masks, astral projection, the zodiac and the Magical Battle of Britain.

Spirit in the City
The supernatural entities that we work with. The elementals of earth, fire, air and water.

If you have enjoyed this book, then look out for:
The Craft in the City (Local Legend, 2012):
ISBN 978-1-907203-43-5

describing in detail the tools of the Craft, candle magic,
how to cleanse and protect with magic salt,
the correspondences between days, planets, herbs, colours and essential oils, the festivals of the year and much more.